W9-BMV-351

The Cradle and the Crown

A Regent College Advent Reader

The Cradle and the Crown

A Regent College Advent Reader

A Medley of Reflections
edited by G. Richard Thompson,
Susan M. Fisher,
and Stacey Gleddiesmith

REGENT COLLEGE PUBLISHING
Vancouver, British Columbia

The Cradle and the Crown:
Regent College Advent Reflections
Copyright © 2006, 2011 G. Richard Thompson,
Susan M. Fisher, and Stacey Gleddiesmith

All rights reserved. No part of this publication may be reproduced, stored in a retrieval system, or transmitted, in any form or by any means, electronic, mechanical, photo-copying, recording or otherwise, without the prior written permission of the author, except in the case of brief quotations embodied in critical articles and reviews.

First edition published 2006
Revised and expanded edition 2011 by Regent College Publishing
5800 University Boulevard, Vancouver, BC V6T 2E4 Canada
Web: www.regentpublishing.com
E-mail: info@regentpublishing.com

Unless otherwise noted, Scripture taken from the
HOLY BIBLE, NEW INTERNATIONAL VERSION®.
Copyright © 2001, 2005 by Biblica®. Used by permission of Biblica®.
All rights reserved worldwide.

Regent College Publishing is an imprint of the Regent Bookstore
<www.regentbookstore.com>. Views expressed in works published by Regent College Publishing are those of the author and do not necessarily represent the official position of Regent College <www.regent-college.edu>.

Library and Archives Canada Cataloguing in Publication

The Cradle and the Crown
Edited by G. Richard Thompson, Susan M. Fisher, and Stacey Gleddiesmith

ISBN 978-1-57383-454-4

1. Christmas—Meditations. 2. Advent—Meditations. I. Thompson, G. Richard (Gordon Richard), 1962–. II. Fisher, Susan M. (Susan Maxine), 1965–. III. Gleddiesmith Stacey, 1975–. IV. Regent College.

BV40 C67 2011   242'.332 22

Contents

Acknowledgments

2006 Edition

I gratefully acknowledge the important contributions of those who made this advent reader a reality. To Regent's Vice President of External Relations, Patti Towler—whose brilliant idea to create an Advent Reader for the Regent community gave birth to this project—and to the members of our External Relations team, thanks for all your support and your behind-the-scenes work. To Bethany Murphy, our copy editor, thank you for your careful and cheerful work in reviewing and compiling the submissions. To Robert Hand of Regent Publishing, thank you for your diligent work and gracious attitude in the face of the tight timeline that we required. To Darrell Johnson, I am deeply grateful for your vision for this project and for the constant inspiration and encouragement that kept us going; your two contributions are fitting bookends to this collection. To Susan Fisher, my co-editor who is far more gifted and experienced at this task of editing than I, thank you for the professionalism and expertise that you brought to this project. And finally, I am very grateful for the forty-five contributors who have written the beautiful and thoughtful reflections found within these pages. You were a delight to work with and I am pleased that this collection displays your giftedness with words, highlights the uniqueness of your personalities, and reflects the diversity that is so characteristic of the Regent community. Thank you and Merry Christmas!

Richard Thompson
Director of Development, Regent College
Regent Alum (ThM, 2000)

Acknowledgments

2011 Edition

When we first began this project, the Advent Reader was a Regent-style thank you to 2006 donors. The reception it received, however, and the increasing popularity of the Advent Reader as we completed our 2007, 2008, and 2010 versions have caused us to revisit our earliest Reader in order to ensure it can be used for every Advent season. To do this, we added the work of twelve new writers; I am very thankful for the energy, passion, and talent with which they approached their various texts. They have worked to the extremely high standards set by the first version of this Reader, and have produced scriptural reflections that are both thoughtful and beautiful. I am also extremely grateful to Rosi Petkova, Regent's very talented Publication Artist, and her able assistant, Ivan Lo, for their patience and skill in layout and design. A complete re-organization of the Reader did not make their job easy. Finally, thank you to Bethany Murphy for her superior copy editing skills, and to Rob Clements of Regent Publishing, who brought the final work to life and spearheaded the addition of an electronic version. We hope that this Advent Reader will draw you into the life and work of Christ each Advent for years to come.

Stacey Gleddiesmith
Bon Accord, Alberta
Freelance Writer and Editor
Regent Alum (MDiv, 2007)

Introduction

You are holding in your hands what we trust will become a precious treasure. In these pages, we, members of the Regent College family, have sat before a text of Holy Scripture and are inviting you in on the responses of our hearts and minds. In particular, we are sharing with you our reflections on some of the biblical passages that a large part of the Christian church reads during the season called "Advent."

The word comes from the Latin *adventus*, simply meaning, "coming." Advent is the season of the Christian year when the church intentionally chooses to move into a "posture of waiting," in two senses. One, choosing to go back and enter again into the space before the first Christmas, awaiting with God's people of old the advent of the Promised One. And two, looking forward and entering into the space of the advent of the Glorious One, when he comes to bring to fulfillment all he came to do in the first advent. The season sharpens for us the two defining horizons of our life in Jesus: living in light of his first coming, when he lived as one of us, healed and taught us the way of *shalom*, was crucified for our sins and won the victory over evil and death; and in light of his second coming, when he makes all things new, when he "will wipe away every tear from their eyes" (Rev. 7:17).

A word or two about how to work with this treasure. Begin by reading the day's biblical text. Before reading the reflection, we encourage you to ask your own questions of the text and to make your own observations. We are trusting that you will then find yourself wanting to pray and worship in a fresh way.

We pray that during this season, as you read with us, our reflections will increase both your wonder at his first advent and your longing for his second. *Maranatha!*

Darrell W. Johnson
Vancouver, BC
Pastor, First Baptist Church
Former Associate Professor, Pastoral Theology
Regent College

Ten-year Schedule for first Sundays of Advent

Start reading on the dates given below for each year.

2011 – November 27
2012 – December 2
2013 – December 1
2014 – November 30
2015 – November 29
2016 – November 27
2017 – December 3
2018 – December 2
2019 – December 1
2020 – November 29

Expectant Waiting ...

Isaiah 25:1–9

Advent began just outside the gate of the Garden of Eden. From the moment Adam and Eve stepped out of perfection and walked into the darkness of the world, they needed to be redeemed.

The people of Israel lived with God's promise that he would send a saviour. The period of waiting must have seemed endless. Add to those feelings the years of exile and the intermittent, prolonged oppression and persecution. Prophets, like Isaiah, continued to assure the people that one day the Messiah would come. Certainly there was enough evidence that God always keeps a promise.

The season of Advent was designed to *remember the waiting* and to provide time for reflection on Jesus' coming in the past, his coming to us each day, and his promise to come again.

Waiting ...
What does that mean?
To wait is to watch in expectation.
Since God requires it, there is purpose in waiting.
Do we *really* expect God to come?
Are we waiting well?

Advent is a gift of time to daily receive the one who is always coming to us.

Martha Zimmerman
Juneau, Alaska
Writer and Author
Guest Lecturer, Regent College

In Both Seasons

Matthew 2:13–23

The book of Matthew begins by slowly and laboriously recounting the Messiah's ancestors. It then launches into a fast and furious explosion of events: Jesus' conception, his birth, and the glorious and fantastic prophecies surrounding the Messiah. Just as suddenly, the story takes a long pause. Between the last verse in chapter 2 and the first verse in chapter 3, nearly three decades pass before Matthew picks up the story again. This long-awaited Messiah has finally come, but all Matthew cares to tell us about his first thirty years is the shockingly sparse, "He went and lived in a town called Nazareth."

This is the way of God: long waiting, intense action, followed by long waiting. Decades may come and go before anything seemingly significant takes place. The Gospels testify to a patient God who sometimes takes centuries to set up his move, and who then thinks nothing of sitting on it for another thirty years until everything is just right.

Is this not also true of God's work in our lives? At times, God's activity will seem intense and glorious. At other times, it may seem as if he is taking a nap. Waiting is, by God's design, a significant part of the Christian life. Sometimes, we will feel as if we are in the center of God's work; at other times, we may feel like all we are doing is living in a simple town. In both seasons, however, we are still living the Life of Christ.

Gary Thomas
Bellingham, Washington
Writer and Author
Regent Alum (MCS, 1988)

A Tender Bud

Isaiah 11:1–10

A tender bud, growing from the root of Jesse, is Isaiah's hope. Hope that the Spirit of God will bring understanding beyond that which is seen with human eyes and heard with human ears. Hope that a child will grow in the knowledge of God to treat the poor with mercy and kindness. Hope for a land of peace and loving-kindness—for who but a child can have faith that the impossible is worth working for?

And we, like Isaiah, know our world aches for a tender bud of hope. People everywhere tremble in fright, cry for help, flee in panic. So with Isaiah we yearn for a tender bud sprouting—with tenacious faith that abundant life is still possible.

And as we yearn, perhaps even we are born into God's kingdom as a tender bud of hope. As the Spirit of God hovers over us, do we hear with our hearts the cry of the oppressed? As the Spirit of God hovers over us, do we, too, find childlike faith to create a land where we do not harm, a land full of peace and loving-kindness?

In this season and always, may the Spirit of God hover over us.

Sarah Craig Freeman
Richmond, Virginia
Director of Development, YMCA
Regent Alum (MCS, 2003)

A Light in Darkness

Isaiah 9:2–7

Darkness. We wait for the promised one in darkness. And we wait not in the beautiful darkness of a moonless night, but in the ugly darkness of a good creation dissolved into chaos. Isaiah saw it as the setting for this prophetic oracle concerning the Promised One: "Distressed and hungry, they will roam through the land; when they are famished, they will become enraged and, looking upward, will curse their king and their God. Then they will look toward the earth and see only distress and darkness and fearful gloom, and they will be thrust into utter darkness" (Isa. 8:21–22).

Darkness seems incompatible with our desire to make the Advent season a time of anticipation and joy for family and friends. Yet this very season of anticipated joys often becomes, for many, a season of darkness—of keenly felt suffering and hopelessness. Despite our inclination to whitewash such inconvenient realities, the prophet will have none of it. Instead, the darkness is fully acknowledged and named.

But darkness does not have the final word. Instead, it becomes the divinely chosen context for the revelation of the Promised One who is to come: *"The people walking in darkness* have seen a great light . . . " (v. 2).

Uli H. Chi
Normandy Park, Washington
Chairman, Computer Human Interaction, LLC
Former Chairman, Board of Directors, Regent College

The Triumph of the Lamb

Revelation 17

Among the images of stars and donkeys, sparkly angels, and shepherds wearing tea towels and old sheets, it's easy to forget that, at the heart, the story of Advent is about two clashing kingdoms and a cosmic struggle for power. It is about the surprising way in which God reclaims his power over creation, disarming the other "powers" that have corrupted it.

Few passages capture this element of Advent as clearly as Revelation 17. Here we meet the glittering "Whore of Babylon" astride her many-headed beast; she is drunk with the blood of God's people and oozes a kind of grotesque beauty—the seductive and corrupting desire for absolute power. Together the beast and the whore broadly represent both the ungodly kingdoms of the world and the demonic powers that stand behind them. In their pursuit for control of the world they have one purpose, which is to wage war against the Lamb; for it is only the Lamb that stands in their way.

Think about that for a moment. If it were not for Jesus, demonic powers and ungodly kingdoms could have their way with the world.

This is the very good news of Advent—no matter how powerful the woman and her beast may look, the Lamb "will triumph over them because he is Lord of lords and King of kings—and with him will be his called, chosen and faithful followers" (v. 14). Christ's coming—quietly, secretly at first—will explode finally into a global victory, and his *shalom* shall reign forever.

Tim Horman
Vancouver, British Columbia
Pastor, UTown Church
Regent Alum (MCS, 2007)

Kiss the Son

Psalm 2

The Christmas season, with its scented candles, sugar cookies, and lightly falling snow, is a subversive substitute for Advent. Christmas announces the birth of the King who has come to take his throne. Psalm 2 reminds us that the kings of the earth are set against this King. The world is not neutral about Jesus. *Nations, peoples, kings, and rulers* are a pretty impressive lot. All too often, we *also* become impressed! But God isn't impressed! He laughs at the world's braggadocio and then calls us to haul our intimidated hearts back before the Lord in prayer. It is there that we become un-impressed with the sheer size and weight of the world of un-faith. Prayer leads us backstage where we talk with the director, see the ropes and counterweights of Revelation-reality, and are reminded that there is one King who rules them all. "To us a son is given, and the government will be on his shoulders" (Isa. 9:6). So *kiss the Son* this Advent and pray your way through all the world's intimidation, past the sugar cookies and scented candles, and *celebrate with trembling* before the King of kings. O, come, let us adore him!

"Thou art coming to a King, large petitions with thee bring,
for his grace and power are such, none can ever ask too much."

Tom Oster
Roanoke, Virginia
Pastor
Regent Alum (MDiv, 1994)

The Pain of Deliverance

Exodus 13

What captivates me about the exodus story—a story that is foundational to our identity as Christian people—is all the moments when Yahweh's deliverance seems like pure drudgery, seems even like pain.

I wonder who said it would be any different for us.

If the narrative of the incarnation highlights anything, it is the posture of self-emptying, *kenosis*, that Christ undertook in order to be born in human likeness. And if Christ's incarnation is foundational for our subsequent deliverance, is there something of this *kenosis* that is required of us on *our* exodus journeys?

See God's people, Israel, hastily leaving Egypt in the night, and notice the pure chaos of the scene. When Yahweh grants you freedom, he doesn't grant it on your time.

See Moses obeying this absurd command—"Stretch out your hand over the sea to divide the water (Exod. 14:16)—and notice how much of himself he must overcome in order to obey.

Watch as the Israelites see "the Egyptians lying dead on the shore" (Exod. 14:30), and understand something of the wounding nature of God's salvation.

Look around you at God's people putting one foot in front of the other as the waters come up to their necks, praying with Hosea, "Come, let us return to the Lord. He has torn us to pieces but he will heal us.... After two days, he will revive us ... that we may live in his presence" (Hos. 6:1–2).

Helen Channer Aupperlee
Grand Rapids, Michigan
Mother and Homemaker
Regent Alum (MDiv, 2007)

God Forges a Path

Isaiah 35

Decorations, holiday music, and Advent celebrations seem to join Isaiah in declaring, "The desert and the parched land will be glad; the wilderness will rejoice and blossom" (v. 1). When the world is in turmoil, and life feels like a wilderness of unmet hope and desert sands, it's easy to recoil from promises and seasons of rejoicing. For many, the celebrating at Christmas time rings false and harsh. If we bear the weight of seemingly unanswered prayers, the collective glee can inflame our thirst for what seems impossible. Yet the Hebrew and Christian promises of God's redemption don't paint God's coming as a "merry" holiday party. God seeks the beloved people where they are, be they in deserts of burning sand or exposed to predators. God, born in flesh and blood, poverty and danger, exile and suffering, knows what it's like to be excluded from celebration and lavish gift-exchanges. God has come to where we are, even when we're on the sidelines, the outskirts, the margins. From wherever we stand on dry and dusty feet, God forges a path, bit by bit, and encourages our steps. On that path, accompanied by God, we might feel a song rise to our lips.

"As with joyful steps they sped, to that lowly manger bed...
So may we with willing feet, ever seek the mercy seat."

Susan S. Phillips
Berkeley, California
Executive Director, New College Berkeley,
Graduate Theological Union
Board of Governors, Regent College

Light in a Small, Dark Room

Psalm 27

Two years ago, at a conference in San Francisco, I met a vibrant twenty-two-year-old Cambodian woman, "Elizabeth." At sixteen, she had been taken by traffickers, kept prisoner in a small, dark room, and forced into prostitution. She wrote Psalm 27 on her wall, and prayed that God would rescue her. Her story pierced me not only with its horror, but because I myself was clinging to Psalm 27 at that time, though not in such grave circumstances.

Even in terrifying difficulty, David reminds us that God is our light and our salvation, the stronghold in which we can weather every storm. No matter if the small dark room we are in is literal, emotional, or even spiritual, we are to seek his beauty and goodness, to dwell continually with him in the shelter of his love.

But the fearless confidence of the Psalmist is also balanced with his pleading call for God to hear and answer him in his distress, because God does not always rescue as we expect, or according to our timetable. For Elizabeth it took eleven long months.

But ultimate rescue is as certain as it is unexpected, brought through Christ's death on the cross. A place of shame and disappointment becomes resurrection and glorious victory. God breaks in, and brings light to even the darkest rooms in our lives.

"Wait for the Lord; be strong and take heart and wait for the Lord."

Nerida Peart
West Pennant Hills, Australia
Assistant Minister, St. Matthew's Anglican Church
Regent Alum (MDiv, 2009)

All Who Sleep in Jesus

1 Thessalonians 4:13–5:11

Reflect on your experiences of death. What funerals or wakes have you attended? Did they inspire your hope in the resurrection? Perhaps not, for in the crush of dark days, hope is sometimes absent. 1 Thessalonians 4:13–5:11 was prompted by concerns for the condition of believers who die before Christ's return. In these verses Paul assures the Thessalonian church that those who have died before the coming again of Jesus will have a share in that glorious event. In writing to correct the thinking of the Thessalonians, Paul has given inspired comfort to the bereaved souls of all believers. Using the language of war, Paul declares victory over death and exhorts us not to lose hope as we put on our battle gear—the breastplate of faith and love and the helmet of the hope of our salvation (5:8). What God did in raising his Son, he is going to do again in raising all who sleep in Jesus. This assurance is based upon the tremendous and undeniable fact of the death and resurrection of Jesus Christ. Mindful of this promise from God's word, let us enter the Advent season with joy as we anticipate the return of the saviour who first came to us as a Bethlehem babe.

Lord, help us always to be prepared for Jesus' second coming.
Help us to remember our heavenly future.

Tony W. Tremblett
Former Technical Services Assistant, Regent Allison Library
Regent Alum (MCS, 2004)

Ready or Not

Revelation 11:15–19

Coming home after a long absence can be a very disarming experience. You make the last turn onto your street; or you open the front door; or you see a loved one's face; or, in my case, you look out across an open wheat field ...

No matter how well prepared you are, you're never really ready for it when it happens. Your throat catches, your eyes fill with tears—you're a mess.

Where does it come from? Why does even the *word* "home" stir a deep sense of longing? Perhaps these experiences awaken the memory of a time and place when you knew that you belonged.

Revelation is not a book about coming home. As with much of the story of God's people, it is a book about *remaining* God's people when we feel far from home, when God seems to have left the building, when humans are behaving like little gods in terrible ways, when we do not seem to belong.

Revelation is God's renewed promise in Jesus that home is coming, or, even better, that our home is already being revealed, and that it is *this* earth. Belonging is not something we return to, but something that God is making, despite our defences, ready or not.

As we remember your cold welcome on this earth,
we thank you for your great power that is redeeming all of creation,
making it evermore our home.
Teach us to be watchful and to participate with you
as we look forward to the day when we will be fully, finally, home.

Cam Tucker
Winnipeg, Manitoba
Software Developer
Regent Alum (MDiv, 2011)

God Breaks In

Isaiah 42:1–9

A sense of exile is inevitable for those who try to live their Christian beliefs faithfully. At times it feels discouraging, even overwhelming, to try to seek righteousness when it requires such counter-cultural thought and action. Sometimes we fail to do much more than the legitimate—the building of houses, the sowing of gardens—and finally we end up accommodating ourselves to the silent gods of Babylon.

But breaking into our exilic state is the living God, he who has stretched out the heavens and spread out the earth. In Isaiah 42 God reminds his people that whatever their present circumstances, they must dare to hope, for through his servant he will bring justice and freedom from exile and shall give sight to the blind and release to those that sit in darkness. Moreover, this hope is not solely for those who know themselves to be in exile, but for those who do not know their plight, who only know that their gods are silent. "I, the LORD, have called you in righteousness; I will take hold of your hand" (v. 6). This is the hope to which we hold, and this is the hope we share.

Sharon Jebb Smith
Aberdeen, Scotland
Teacher and Lecturer
Regent Alum (MCS, 2000)

Unto Us a Child Is Born, Unto Us a Son Is Given

Psalm 104

I yearn to fling my soul into the season of Advent, to rejoice in Christ's birth. Instead, I have wept on my knees in front of the crèche, praying for a more grateful heart; but whenever the newborn baby Jesus becomes the focus of Advent, it magnifies for me, as it does for so many others, a profound source of pain: childlessness.

For several years, I could only read the first line of Psalm 104, "Praise the LORD, my soul," as a command. I could not read it as a joyous exclamation.

But I have my own angels, shepherds, and wise men (friends, pastors, teachers) who point beyond the source of my pain, saying, "Behold, behold!" while God holds the part of me that grieves, whispering constantly, "It's okay, it's okay. I know, I know."

So, gradually, I am learning to read the first line of this psalm as an invitation into the full breadth of Advent. We celebrate much more than the singularly wonderful birth of Jesus. Advent invites us, as we reflect on the whole of this psalm, into relationship with the Trinity. It invites us to remember that the Jesus who was born in Bethlehem, and the Jesus whose return we await, participated in each of the works of creation described by the psalmist.

Our souls need to linger in the light of this psalm, bathe in its waters, confident that, even as a newborn, Jesus is our Creator, our Messiah, and the one who sustains all life. And now we wait for him to come again.

Praise the Lord, my soul.

Susan M. Fisher
Vancouver, British Columbia
Freelance Writer and Editor
Regent Alum (DipCS, 2008)

The Trusting Servant

Isaiah 50:4–11

I often read this passage over the shoulders of the original audience and of Jesus himself, as though I am the servant being addressed. I know, in at least some small measure, what it is to have an *instructed tongue*, an *awakened mind*, and *opened ears*—all to the end of speaking a "word that sustains the weary" (vv. 4–5). Reading on in the passage, however, my appropriation of the text drops away as I recognize with reverence and grief the humiliated and beaten one who is the Suffering Servant.

Echoes from this passage abound in the New Testament. Jesus' withdrawal into quiet places for prayer (Luke 5:16) and his resolute face set toward Jerusalem as his earthly ministry draws to a close (Luke 9:51); descriptions of Jesus' physical suffering during his trial and crucifixion; and the apostle Paul's rhetorical question: "Who will bring any charge against those whom God has chosen?" (Rom. 8:31–34)—all stem from this prophetic passage, encompassing as it does so many aspects of Jesus' ministry.

The passage ends with a stern exhortation. The example of this One—the Instructed Servant, the Listening-Before-Speaking Servant, the Early-Rising Servant, the Resolutely Obedient Servant, the Suffering Servant—rebukes any shortcuts on the path of obedience. We are encouraged to accept times of darkness and suffering as the Perfect Servant does: in trustful obedience to—and full reliance on—a God whose perfect will is being worked out. Even in the dark.

Maxine Hancock
Professor Emerita, Interdisciplinary Studies and Spiritual Theology
Regent College

Fullness of Time

Galatians 4:4–7

In these words from Galatians, perhaps the earliest book of the New Testament, Paul captures the significance of the incarnation. Paul knew much about the depth of human evil from his own times and from within his own self. He also, writing under the influence of the Spirit, had an inkling of the suffering and depravity in those times before when all of humanity was held captive in slavery. But he could not have known the *breadth* of human suffering, tragedy, and depravity that had gone before him over countless millennia. He had no knowledge of the agony of the young African mother, say 20,000 years previous, whose newborn twins were carried off to be exposed by elders of the clan out of superstition; or the anxiety of a young warrior in Europe, 10,000 years before, who was about to be initiated into the art of killing. We now know something of both the depth and breadth of the human tragedy. Like Job we cannot explain the meaning of suffering. But through the Spirit we are conscious that we live within that *fullness of time* and can cry out, "*Abba*, Father" and draw near unto our God, who sent his very Son.

"*Of the Father's love begotten*
Ere the worlds began to be,
He is Alpha and Omega,
He the source, the Ending he,
Of the things that are, that have been,
And that future years shall see,
Evermore and evermore."
(from the Latin of Prudentius)

Bill Reimer
Manager, Regent College Bookstore
Regent Alum (MCS, 2000)

Hints of Radiance
Isaiah 60:1–3

As a child, I dreamed of intact families, realized ideals, wars with endings, and having all the answers. Needless to say, I experienced a rude awakening into adulthood that quickly went beyond my own disappointments. I had only to gulp down a week's worth of global news to digest despair and powerlessness. It is rare to hear of a broken marriage mended, cancer's violence restrained, a neighbourhood redeveloped, or political peace restored. I thirst not only for my own redemption, but also for the larger pieces of healing needed in all realms of creational life and society.

In Isaiah 60:1–3, God acknowledges this potent darkness and confronts it with his own glory. This is where the story is easier for me to *sense* than to know. I see blinding brightness and hear gasps of surprise. I feel heat and warmth at the thought of his entrance and my chest swells with deep breath and wordless joy. I am struck by my forgetfulness of all that was suffocating. Here he is, fiercely shoving out the darkness with his presence alone. We will dance and belly-laugh, in spite of ourselves. Of *course* nations will come—like iron to a magnet. How could they resist such radiance?

Renée D. Swanson
Beaver Falls, Pennsylvania
Stay-at-home Mother and Community Volunteer
President's Assistant, Regent College (1998–2000)

Sing to the Lord

Psalm 98

"Sing to the Lord a new song" begins Psalm 98. But can we sing joyfully this Christmas as we are bombarded with news of violence? Nations are at the brink of war; travelers are at risk of terrorist attacks; our schools have been scenes of senseless violence. The psalmist, as it turns out, is not unacquainted with violence. Ancient Israel was surrounded by enemies, was at times conquered and even taken captive into slavery. What particular, wonderful thing can the psalmist help us sing about this Christmas? None other than the revelation of God's salvation, gained by his holy arm.

This is revealed not just to Israel, but to all the ends of the earth. The enemies of Israel can be expected to tremble in fear. But no, all the earth is exhorted to sing and shout for joy. We are not merely to praise with God-made instruments, our vocal chords, but also with human-made musical instruments. And we humans are not alone in making joyful noise. The choir includes the sea and everything in it, the world and all who live in it, the rivers and the mountains—in short, all of God's creation. Our fuel-depleted, increasingly feverish earth is enjoined to sing. Endangered forests and animals are to clap their hands. And all humanity who desires a just judge are called to praise.

Christmas is a reminder that in answer to our cry for deliverance from evil and a future for our planet, God has unveiled his Salvation through Jesus.

Wan Phek How
Information Systems Director, Regent College
Regent Alum (MCS, 2006)

Hope Itself is Born
Psalm 96

H ere is a rousing call to worship, if ever there was one. The summons to worship reverberates throughout the psalm: proclaim, declare, ascribe, and—repeatedly—sing. But it is a command that is sometimes difficult to obey, for the circumstances of life can sometimes seem to choke us, making our praise catch in our throats. In the middle of the eighteenth century, Anne Steele, the reclusive daughter of an English village pastor, took up her pen and made her attempt to sing a new song. Despite painful personal losses resulting from chronic illness and the deaths of those dearest to her—losses which brought her to the edge of despair as she contemplated life as a "disastrous journey" marked by "pain and grief"—Steele wrote hymns in praise of God. And Christmas tells us how. For into the middle of these times of trouble that may threaten to quell our praise comes God incarnate, the Word itself made flesh. Christ has entered "this dark Wilderness, this vale of tears," and his birth is attended by another—hope itself is born. Here is a reason to sing, with Steele, a new song:

"Wrap'd in the gloom of dark despair, We helpless, hopeless lay:
But sovereign mercy reach'd us there, And smil'd despair away."

Cindy Aalders
Doctoral Candidate, Oxford
Former Assistant Registrar, Regent College
Regent Alum (MCS, 2002)

Our Sympathetic High Priest

Hebrews 4:14–16

"**I** know what you're going through." When these words are not used merely as a platitude but instead ring with truth, they can have the power to heal, comfort, and affirm us in our darkest moments of pain and suffering. It's the simple knowledge that someone else can fully understand your pain because they have tasted it for themselves.

Hebrews 4 reminds us that God can speak those words truthfully in every circumstance.

Traditionally, a high priest would intercede between the people and God. Yet the priests were themselves sinners, their access to God was limited, and the sympathy they were able to offer was imperfect. But we have a great High Priest who is not bound by these restrictions. One who knows the reality of our lives, and enters into the messiness of life with us, without judgment or accusation. In Jesus we have a perfect, sufficient, and eternal High Priest who can relate to our suffering because he has fully experienced it himself.

God did not need a lesson in suffering. God's embracing of human form was for *our* benefit—so we could truly comprehend that we have a God who is intimately acquainted with our grief.

Lord, grant us your strength to endure our times of suffering,
that we might also be able to understand and help bear the
burdens of those around us.
May we hold fast to your promises in these storms of life,
and see your faithfulness in all circumstances.

Jude Trenier
London, England
Executive Director, FACE Youth
Former Student (2006–2007)

Comfort!

Isaiah 40:1-11

The magnificence of Christ's coming is matched only by the squalor of the broken world into which he chooses to be born: a lowly stable's harsh textures, sounds, and smells. Crowds press in on that first Advent, the inn fills quickly, and rejection stings the young woman with child as her hapless husband holds her upon a tired donkey. Such a scene resonates with every living person whose luck has ever run dry. What kind of entrance can this be for the Messiah? Why would God send his Son in such an unlikely fashion? For Isaiah, the answer is found in one word: *comfort!* In Christ, God chooses to comfort wounded persons, hostages to sin's bleak devastation. Comfort on such a scale requires a radical redemption. And God enters fully into our sorrow. He did so then; he does so now. In Advent, the kindness of God is writ large for us as we await the Saviour's birth, for he extends comfort to the wounded spirit. Advent's invitation reads: *rest in my love, relax in my care, trust me with your pain, and accept my comfort.* As we receive Jesus, God personally reveals his glory through his comfort and redemption.

Throughout this Advent season, Gracious God,
fill our hearts with your comfort and joy,
releasing those held hostage to past regrets and future fears.
In these quiet days of anticipating the Christ child's coming,
embrace us with your sure and certain hope, in the Saviour's name,
Amen.

Paul M. Beckingham
Assistant Professor of Church and Mission
Carey Theological College
Regent Alum (MDiv, 1993)

Humiliation and Humility

Matthew 27:27–31

The sheer injustice and cruelty shown in this scene, to an innocent man, to the Messiah, is too much to take. He seems as weak and helpless as the day he was born.

Yet Jesus is a long way from his birth in a backwater town, out back in a manger. Barely anyone noticed him then. A select few—the poor, the outcasts, the foreigners—came to bow beside his manger in wonder. Things are a little different now. Now, at the age of thirty-three, he's drawn the wrath of pretty much every authority figure in Jerusalem.

The events of Jesus' birth and death are so different from each other. But in each we see how Jesus has set aside the power rightfully available to him—first, taking the form of a human being, a baby, and later submitting to cruel mockery and crucifixion. Who could have imagined a Saviour that would allow himself to be subjected to any of this?

But it is through this deliberate relinquishment of power, this seeming weakness, that we see just how powerful Jesus is, how he conquers death and the powers-that-be. This scene of humiliation at the hands of the soldiers, this horrible parody of worship, is merely foreshadowing the glorious day that will come when "at the name of Jesus every knee [will] bow, in heaven and on earth and under the earth, and every tongue acknowledge that Jesus Christ is Lord, to the glory of God the Father" (Phil. 2:10–11).

Audrey Molina
San Francisco, California
Communications Associate
Regent Alum (MCS, 2006)

Pothole Theology

Isaiah 49:1–6

A re you in a pothole? Being perplexed is a normal Christian experience (2 Cor. 4:7–12). When Abraham left everything behind and ventured by faith to the promised land, God afflicted that land with a famine. Tragically, Abraham, unlike our Lord, turned stones in the promised land into bread, outside of God's will. Eating bread in Egypt almost cost Abraham his life and his wife's purity. Moses first embraced the hardness of Pharaoh's heart before saving Israel. And Christ and his apostles embraced to death the hardness of the Jewish authorities and the Roman Empire.

Do you want to be lifted out of your pothole? The dialogue between God and his anonymous servant—fulfilled in Jesus Christ—aims to empower us. The servant is as capable of establishing God's kingdom by his speaking as a sharp sword and polished arrow to win the battle. But he remains hidden and unused (vv. 1–2). Moreover, he exhausted himself to fulfill his mission to restore Israel to God, but has nothing to show for his labour (v. 4a). But the servant triumphed, for he knew that God would honour him (v. 5b) and that God must reward his efforts (v. 4b). As it turned out, through Israel's rejection of him he accomplished something far greater: he brought salvation to the world (v. 6).

So don't lose heart. As you give your life for Christ, remember that it is a sweet savour to God and a perfume to the world. Count on God, not mortals, to reward you.

Bruce Waltke
Professor Emeritus, Old Testament Studies
Regent College

Nature or Nurture?

Micah 5:2–5

I remember the summer it happened. I went from being the average height, plus-size, chunky girl to the tallest person in our junior high—jumping hurdles and buying longer pants.

The only girl—the youngest, considered the runt—among three strong, handsome, and athletic older brothers whom I adored and endured. But in one summer I surpassed everyone: Mom, Dad, Larry, Ron, and Steve, both Grandmas, and one Grandpa. Stepping solidly into the image, at that point unseen, of my birth family tree; highlighting differences that had not yet been so obvious. Going from runt status to 5'10" brought new power over my brothers and forced me to step into my own DNA. It also brought a strange feeling of mis-fitting in the only family I had known. Though having nothing to do with my physical posture, my adoptive family had much to do with nurturing my own emotional and spiritual journey to stand tall.

In many ways Jesus surprised everybody, maybe even himself. Growing into a strength and a calling most did not expect from the smallest among the clans. I have to wonder if he struggled sometimes as he grew into his calling and his shepherd-rule. Knowing something of the tension of wanting to fit in *and* step into his DNA, I believe he knows me too. And so I wait to ask him . . . nature or nurture? I think he'd say, "Yes."

Lani F. Parker
Edmonds, Washington
Former Director, Regent College Foundation USA

Unexpected Blessing

Acts 17:1–9

Disappointment, rejection, unmet expectations—whatever you choose to call it, being let down is not a pleasant experience. This is especially true when it involves something we really want. The pain of these experiences makes us want to avoid them at all costs, lest we succumb to despair.

This is the situation that we find in Acts 17.

Paul has just explained that Jesus is the expected Messiah. Despite this good news, many of the Jews did not embrace his message. This sounds quite surprising at first. Wouldn't every Jew be excited to hear that their Messiah has finally come?

Luke tells us that Paul proved to them, using their own Scriptures, that the Messiah must suffer and die. Imagine how that would sound. They had waited hundreds of years for the Messiah to conquer their foes and restore them to prominence, only to find out that his victory wouldn't include the imperial dominance they had come to expect.

It is tempting to dismiss the Jews in this story for their obstinate refusal of such good news. But perhaps we, too, are tempted to hold too tightly to things we want. Perhaps we, too, expect God to act in certain ways, according to certain patterns. Fortunately, as we learn here and elsewhere in Scripture, when people let go of the things they want, God is able to give them something far greater. As we wait during this season of Advent, may we, too, be open to God's unexpected blessings.

Russell Pinson
Head of Operations, Marketplace Institute
Regent College
Regent Alum (MCS, 2009)

A Fondness for Foolishness

1 Corinthians 1:18–25

The essence of humour is incongruity. When we recognize something that is ridiculous or out of place, like animals in human clothing or people taking a frivolous thing seriously, we can't help but laugh.

The more seriously we take ourselves, however, the more trouble we have recognizing humour.

As so often happens to us, the Corinthian church had begun taking themselves too seriously. They wanted to be known for their dignified wisdom. They had broken into warring groups, each with their chests puffed out as far as they could go, insisting that the others were not up to snuff. In the midst of this self-righteous posturing, Paul pointed out that the one they claimed to worship had died the most humiliating death they could imagine. He showed them how ridiculous it was to take themselves seriously when the message of the cross is foolishness to the world.

Just as there is incongruity in worshiping a crucified man, there is also incongruity in the incarnation. The God of the universe who died a humiliating death first suffered a humiliating birth. The life, death, and even the resurrection of Jesus is a satire directed at all of us, forcing us to recognize that God is willing to be more foolish than we are. We would probably have chosen a more dignified way of saving the world. But then, we are not as fond of foolishness as God is.

Elliot Ritzema
Bellingham, Washington
Editor, Logos Bible Software
Regent Alum (MDiv, 2008)

A Divine Model

Philippians 2:1–11

Paul didn't know about Christmas, but he did know well the event that Christmas should be all about: the incarnation of the eternal God in the person of the Son. The truly striking thing is that this marvellous telling of Christ's story exists not for theological reasons—an attempt to demonstrate his deity—but for very practical ones, to offer a divine model in contrast to the selfish ambition and vain conceit in verse 3. The incarnation part of the story (vv. 6–8) is thus told in two sentences, the basic elements of which tell us the following: as God he poured himself out by taking the form of a slave (vv. 6–7a, vis-à-vis "selfish ambition"); as man he humbled himself by obediently going to the cross (vv. 7b–8, vis-à-vis "vain glory"). And this is the only God there is(!)—in stark contrast to all the grasping, rapacious deities of the pagan cultures into which he was born. The good news is that God is not like us, selfish creatures that we are; rather, he is most fully revealed in the Son's taking the role of a slave, dying for us out of love. And all of this so that we, by his grace, might get our act together!

"This is our God, the Servant King, he calls us now to follow him, to bring our lives as a daily offering of worship to the Servant King."

Gordon D. Fee
Professor Emeritus, New Testament Studies
Regent College

Freedom

Isaiah 61

The prophet Isaiah, looking ahead to the captivity, announces good news to the exiles in Babylon. He proclaims a great reversal: the broken-hearted will be bandaged and healed, the captives will be freed, and the prisoners released. God's people will experience the time of the Lord's favour.

Hundreds of years later, the Lord Jesus comes to the synagogue at Nazareth, reads aloud these words from Isaiah, and says to the people, "Today this scripture is fulfilled ..." (Luke 4:16–21). In the ministry of Jesus the words of the prophet find their deepest and truest fulfillment. One greater than Isaiah has come, and he proclaims a reversal greater than the literal release from Babylonian captivity. The Messiah has come, and he will bring freedom to long-imprisoned spirits, recovery of sight to sin-blinded eyes, release and pardon to sin-oppressed souls. The King has come, and in his kingdom the poor and those who mourn are blessed. He will comfort those who mourn; turn grief into gladness; transform a spirit of dullness, depression, and despair into a heart full of praise. Ruined lives will be restored, renewed. Those who were once far away, foreigners to the covenants of promise, will be brought near. All the people of his kingdom will be priests, proclaiming the praises of him who called us out of darkness into his marvellous light. Immanuel has come to us; in glad response we come to him.

"Out of my bondage, sorrow and night, Jesus, I come, Jesus, I come;
Into Thy freedom, gladness and light, Jesus, I come to Thee."

Doris Evanson
Sessional Lecturer
Regent College

31

God Has Spoken

Hebrews 1:1–14

In Ingmar Bergman's film, *The Seventh Seal*, the medieval knight returning from the Crusades cries out in despair, "I want God to stretch out his hand toward me, reveal himself, speak to me." But he seems to hear nothing. Yet, according to the writer of Hebrews, that's exactly what God has done—namely, speak. Francis Schaeffer summarized it well in the title of his book, *He is There and He Is Not Silent*, as did former Regent professor Klaus Bockmuehl in his book *Listening to the God Who Speaks*.

But how has God spoken? Hebrews answers that though in times past God spoke through the prophets, in this final age he has spoken to us through his Son, who shares all the attributes of deity. He is the heir of all things. He is the creator of the world. He is the radiance of God's glory. He is the exact representation of God's being. He upholds all things by his powerful word. He provided purification for sins. And he was exalted to the right hand of God. This being the case, the Son is certainly superior to angels, readily demonstrated by virtue of his name (vv. 4–5), his dignity (v. 5), his nature (vv. 7–12), and his status (vv. 13–14). He is and has done all this for us, the heirs of salvation (v. 14).

Sven Söderlund
Professor Emeritus, Biblical Studies
Regent College

Violence and Grace

Isaiah 63:1–6

For many, the Advent season offers a solace from the barrage of reports of bloodshed and violence that surround us. We quiet our souls in anticipation of the coming of the Prince of Peace. But soon we find our senses disturbed by gory images that often accompany the salvation narrative. Isaiah 63:1–6 describes a righteous God "mighty to save" (v. 1), but who accomplishes salvation by trampling his enemies with such wrath that their blood is spattered on his garments (v. 3). This imagery reminds us of Christ, the conquering Son who dons "a robe dipped in blood" (Rev. 19:13). How are we to make sense of these violent images? We can start by revising our domesticated image of God. For the God of love is also the God of wrath. We learn too that judgment is a necessary condition for salvation. By divine grace, the violence that we, as God's enemies, ought to have suffered was borne for us by our Saviour. The divine hospitality extended to us comes at the cost of divine violence suffered on our behalf. And divine violence will have its last word; it will bring an end to all the violence and bloodshed in the world.

Almighty and gracious Lord, create in us a healthy
and reverential fear of You. Amen.

How Chuang Chua
Deerfield, Illinois
Missionary to Japan, OMF International
Regent Alum (ThM, 1997)

The Coming King

Numbers 24:15–19

Balaam's previous oracles anticipate a royal figure with both divine and human associations (Num. 23:21; 24:7). This fourth oracle develops the expectation of a mysterious coming ruler by means of two metaphors. The "star" was widely associated with supernatural beings (e.g., Amos 5:26). The "sceptre" (or "rod") symbolized the power of rulers, whether exercised oppressively (e.g., Isa. 9:4) or for discipline and protection (e.g., Ps. 2:9; Isa. 11:4). The motif of dominion recurs in Numbers 24:19 (cf. Ps. 110:2).

The war-like connotations of the royal "sceptre" are similarly anticipated in the previous oracles. These connotations are elaborated in the battle imagery of Numbers 24:17–19: the striking of the enemies' heads, in particular, links this passage to later expressions of victory over God's enemies (e.g., Ps. 110:5–6).

In a remarkable yet familiar way, these threads of prophetic foresight are woven together into a tapestry that finds coherence and completeness in Jesus, a garment that conforms to him alone. He is the Lion of the tribe of Judah (Rev. 5:5). He is the bright Morning Star (Rev. 22:16). To him belongs the sceptre of iron (Rev. 19:15). To him belongs eternal dominion (Rev. 5:12–13). He it is who, born on earth amidst conflict and bloodshed, will return in conquest, the King of kings from heaven (Rev. 12:5; 17:14; 19:12).

"Joy to the world, the Lord is come. Let earth receive her king."

David M. Clemens
Adjunct Professor, Biblical Languages
Regent College

Christ the Gardener

Genesis 2:4–25

A dvent is a time to reflect on Jesus' first and second comings; however, it's not often thought of as related to Genesis. But of course the creation story has Christ's fingerprints all over it, for all things were created through him.

I have recently been listening to Paul Spicer's fascinating "Easter Oratorio" (2000). The words (by N. T. Wright) are ingenious, interweaving the resurrection narrative with the creation account: "The garden of creation / was Adam's glad employ; / the garden of redemption / is Jesus' right and joy . . . / The new creation wakens / before his skilful hand; / The thorns and thistles vanish / At Jesus' royal command."

Reading Genesis 2:4–25 with this in mind opens up a whole new understanding. The Lord Jesus enters the story as the one forming the trees and animals for the man, giving a boundary with respect to the one and a freedom-responsibility with respect to the other, providing a companion who is *bone of his bone* . . .

As we prepare for Christmas, we look back to Jesus' birth when he became *flesh of our flesh*, and we look forward to that garden with the tree of life that he is cultivating for us even now.

"Lord, Thou knowest both the flowers and
the fruits of my garden. . . .
Come and teach me that I grow what will please you most."
(Sr. Josepha Menendez, *The Way of Divine Love*)

Rosie Perera
Vancouver, British Columbia
Writer, Teacher, and Photographer
Regent Alum (MCS, 2004)

Creator and Redeemer

Colossians 1:15–20

For Advent, we take out our songbooks and start singing hymns. Our instinct is exactly right. When St. Paul starts talking about the coming of Christ, he, too, bursts into song. This passage, one of the most ancient Christian hymns, is the outcome of the apostle's urge to sing praise to the one who became flesh on Christmas Day. One item is particularly worth pondering in this song: it is the twofold title that Paul gives to the Son of God. He is both the "firstborn over all creation" (v. 15) and he is the "firstborn from among the dead" (v. 18). Christmas has to do with both. We rightly sing because of the second title. Incarnation *leads* to cross and resurrection, and so to redemption and peace. As firstborn from among the dead, Christ is our redeemer. But we should not forget to sing also because of the first title, for it is the "firstborn over all creation" who *becomes* incarnate. The story of Advent only makes sense against the backdrop of eternity. The only reason why the "firstborn from among the dead" is able to bring salvation is that he is also the "firstborn over all creation." He is redeemer of the world only because he is also its creator.

Gracious Lord, we praise you for your marvellous grace.
That you, the creator of the world,
should come to us, to redeem us!
That in and through yourself you should raise us to eternal life!
Again, we wait for you, our Alpha and Omega,
our beginning and our end. Amen.

Hans Boersma
J.I. Packer Professor of Theology
Regent College

Son of David

2 Samuel 7:4–17

The Lord's remarkable promise to King David recorded in 2 Samuel 7:4–17 (cf. 1 Chron. 17:3–15) may justifiably be described as the theological pinnacle of the Old Testament. With pledges such as "I will make your name great" (v. 9) and "I will provide a place for my people Israel" (v. 10), the Davidic promise of 2 Samuel 7 recalls the covenant first made with Abraham (Gen. 12:1–3) and refocuses it on David. And with pledges such as "I will establish the throne of his kingdom forever" (v. 13) and "I will be his father, and he will be my son" (v. 14), it anticipates the messianic hope that becomes increasingly dominant in the pages of the Old Testament and finds its ultimate fulfillment in the advent of "Jesus the Messiah the son of David, the son of Abraham" (Matt. 1:1).

David wanted to do something for God; but God insisted, rather, on involving David in something wonderful that he was doing for David—and ultimately for us! In and through Jesus, the greater son of David, we are brought into a "kingdom [that] will endure forever" (v. 16). To such grace we can only respond as David did: "How great you are, O Sovereign LORD!" (2 Sam. 7:22).

Lord, how astonishing is your care for your people.
Though we might wish to do something for you,
you ever outdo us with blessings that
we could never have anticipated
and can never repay. Thank you!

V. Philips Long
Professor, Old Testament
Regent College

Christmas: Better Than It Has to Be

Daniel 7

Christmas is extravagance. Already well provisioned, we prepare special foods in special quantities. We decorate rooms already furnished and decorated. We give each other gifts—and decorate them, too. From such happy thoughts we turn to a tale that begins in nightmare and ends in terror.

Advent celebrates God dealing with bloody reality. In a world of chimerical kingdoms combining good and evil, and of often bestial ruthlessness and arrogance, God asserts his reign. The Ancient of Days sets up his court, opens his books, and metes out judgment. There is a God in heaven who deals with Babylon, Persia, Augustus, Herod, and everyone else who dominates and destroys.

This is good news. But the good news gets much better. For the Almighty, himself an awesome figure, rules through one like a son of man, a human being, an approachable figure because he is not only with us, but like us. And this extravagant good news gets better still. For the rescued earth is ruled—not only by the Ancient of Days, through his deputy the Son of Man—but also by his holy ones, the ones dedicated to his service: namely, us. This is marvel upon marvel.

Self-indulgence and waste at any time is sin. But extravagance at Christmas to celebrate good news that is far, far better than it has to be? It's only fitting.

O Generosity Itself: We stand trembling, agape,
as we stare at the Christ child.
Thank you, now and forever, for your inexpressible gift!

John G. Stackhouse, Jr.
Sangwoo Youtong Chee Professor of Theology and Culture
Regent College

Proclamation of Peace

Isaiah 52:1–12

Peace has been proclaimed? Look out my window, and there's a world ravaged by violence and hatred. Look at my mirror, and there's a soul beset by anxiety and fears. Peace has been proclaimed, really? Look to the mountains of Isaiah 52 and see beautiful feet carrying a beautiful messenger bearing beautiful news— "Your God reigns!" (v. 7). Look to first-century Galilee and see a young carpenter turned rabbi proclaiming "The kingdom of God has come near…believe the good news!" (Mark 1:15). I want to believe, really I do, but…my window…my mirror …

Look again to Isaiah's mountains to see those beautiful feet bringing good news. Are those the same feet that walked the dusty roads of Galilee? The same ones that were nailed to a Roman cross just outside Jerusalem? If so, then that would mean that the Lord has come to Zion just as he promised! And we have seen it with our own eyes (1 Cor. 15:1–8)! But…what about my window, my mirror?

And so we long and we wait for his return, when the reign he inaugurated at his first advent shall be fully revealed. At that time we shall shake off our dust and burst into song like never before! Yet he *has* come. He *is* Immanuel. And he *has* brought us peace.

"Go, tell it on the mountain, over the hills and everywhere.
Go, tell it on the mountain that Jesus Christ is born."

Richard Thompson
Director of Development, Regent College
Regent Alum (ThM, 2000)

fear Not!

Luke 2:8–20

We live in a culture filled with all kinds of fears. Luke 2:8–20 gives us reason not to fear, for the text reveals the character of the Triune God, incarnate in Jesus, whose perfect love casts out all fear.

An angel urged the shepherds to "fear not!" because of the great good news of Christ's birth. God's incarnation changed the cosmos, for inherent in Christ's becoming flesh was his obedient life, teaching, ministry, death, and resurrection for us. This is the greatest joy and hope for all people: a Saviour who rescues us from ourselves, a Messiah who accomplishes God's purposes, a Lord in submission to whom we experience true life.

The child is born in David's city—a fulfillment of God's promise and verification (continually reaffirmed in Christ's work) that God will unceasingly keep his promises. We are even given a sign: the humility of God's infancy and the poverty of a manger birthplace. We need not fear poverty or oppression; Jesus went through them and conquered them.

God is glorified and peace is bequeathed. How can we help but join the shepherds and Mary in proclaiming, pondering, and praising?

"Come, Thou long-expected Jesus, born to set thy people free;
from our fears and sins release us; let us find our rest in thee."

Marva J. Dawn
Vancouver, Washington
Teaching Fellow, Spiritual Theology
Regent College

The Poverty of Christ

2 Corinthians 8:9

These thirty words sum up the meaning of Christmas as well as any in the Bible. Yet Paul wrote them as part of a very lowly genre, an appeal for money. He was trying to persuade the Christians in Corinth (which was a wealthy trading city) to send some of their bounty to the poverty-stricken Jewish Christians in Jerusalem. Paul, an educated Jew, knew better than anyone what it meant for Gentiles now to be graciously included in that story of renewed creation which had long been experienced by the descendants of Abraham.

So to make his point, Paul reminds the comfortable Christians at Corinth of the central Christian mystery. The "poverty" he describes is not Jesus' modest means as a traveling prophet, preacher, and healer. It is rather the poverty of the self-giving God who "emptied himself," whom we meet fully in Jesus, through whom (as Paul had written in an earlier letter) "all things came and through whom we live" (1 Cor. 8:6). Thus the "poverty" of Jesus is the love of the Creator whom we meet on the cross, who makes us his image-bearing creatures—and who, through Christ and in the Spirit, is making us his new creatures.

"Drained is love in making full, bound in setting others free;
poor in keeping many rich, weak in giving power to be."
(W. H. Vanstone)

Loren E. Wilkinson
Professor, Interdisciplinary Studies and Philosophy
Regent College

41

God Sent His Son

John 3:13–21

In talking with Nicodemus, Jesus compares himself to the bronze snake that Moses lifted in the desert. Numbers 21:4–9 describes how the Israelites petulantly grumble against God, pining away for the "good ol' days" in Egypt. To remind the people of what life was really like in Egypt, God sends deadly snakes, reminiscent of the serpent that Pharaoh wore on his headpiece.

The Israelites repent and ask Moses to petition the Lord to take the snakes away. Instead of doing what was requested, God directs Moses to make another snake, raise it on a pole, and instruct anyone who is bitten to look at it and live. God doesn't remove the snakes; he provides a way of healing for those who are bitten.

So often we, too, ask God to take something away, whether a difficult circumstance or a particular struggle with sin. We fixate on our problems, complaining that God doesn't care. God's answer is to send his Son into the world to bring salvation, the ultimate healing. God calls us to place our faith in his one and only Son who was lifted up, that whoever believes in him will not perish but have eternal life.

Lord, fix our eyes on you, that we may receive your salvation.

Toni Huang Kim
Boston, Massachusetts
Minister of Adult Education, Park Street Church
Regent Alum (MCS, 1998)

A Conflicting Kingdom

Matthew 16:13–28

Every year, on November 1, Canadian storeowners trade in their Halloween paraphernalia for Christmas décor, marking the beginning of the consumer's Christmas season. Subsequently, it is impossible to leave home without being assaulted by the blitzkrieg of advertisements aiming to convince us that if we buy a certain product, we will actualize the love, security, peace, and joy we ache for. Advent calls us away from this frenzy, summoning us to commemorate the birth of Jesus and to focus with anticipation on Christ's second coming and the full establishment of his kingdom.

In Matthew 16:13–28, we are reminded that Jesus' kingdom conflicts with the expectations placed upon him by those who love and seek to follow him. Peter's tone shifts from declaring Jesus as Messiah to sternly rebuking Jesus for teaching that the cross is central to his kingship. Ironically, Peter does not desire to submit himself to the way of the one he acknowledges as king.

This story reinforces the fact that Jesus' kingship embraces vulnerability. In the incarnation, God embraced humanity to share in our vulnerability—even unto death—so that we may share in the glory of his resurrection. This is the true gift that we are to remember, celebrate, and anticipate in the days leading up to Christmas—the true gift worthy of the entirety of our attention and devotion. Advent not only exposes the ludicrousness of chasing after the treasures of the world, but also invites us to prepare our hearts to continue to receive the fullness of the gift of God incarnate.

Adam Greeley
Halifax, Nova Scotia
Pastor, Gateway Community Church
Regent Alum (MDiv, 2010)

The Story of Two Kings
Luke 2:1–7

The Christ-mas story is a story about two kings. In Rome, we find Caesar Augustus, the greatest of the Roman emperors, well known for his passion for power and glory. He had changed his named from Octavian to Augustus, "the one to be honoured," and he strongly promoted the cult of the deified Julius Caesar. As part of his strategy to demonstrate supreme power, he had issued a decree that a census should be taken of the entire Roman world. He craved even more dominance and control.

The other king is just about to enter the world. Neither in Rome, nor in Jerusalem, but in the outer margins of the current Roman and Jewish society, far from majesty and glory, palaces and celebrities. We read about a poor and unmarried teenage girl who gives birth to a child. And there was no room for them.

In the end, this is a story about two fundamentally different ways of manifesting power: from above or from below, in strength or in weakness, a mighty ruler versus a defenceless baby. When God is about to manifest his power and presence in the world, he contradicts all human expectation concerning wisdom and strength. God does it his own way.

Where will this God find room today?

Mikael Tellbe
Örebro, Sweden
Lecturer, New Testament Studies, Örebro Theological Seminary
Regent Alum (ThM, 1993)

Expecting Glory

Matthew 17:1–13

This passage has it all: Jesus transforms before the disciples' eyes, clothing as bright as light, face like the sun; he is a figure out of apocalyptic mythology speaking to two long-dead prophets. This, surely, is what the reign of God on earth should consist of! No wonder Peter offers to build tabernacles on the mountaintop.

Then comes the shining cloud, sign of God's presence throughout the Old Testament, and the Father affirms Jesus and warns the disciples to "listen to him" (v. 5). And with that, everything turns on its head: they come down the mountain alone with a "normal" Jesus who, as they listen, begins reconfiguring every expectation they had of his role. First, he warns them not to talk about this event until after "the Son of Man has been raised from the dead" (v. 9)—a strange time frame to any Jew of that era, and even stranger considering what the disciples had just seen.

Then, when they ask him about Elijah, Jesus turns the conversation to John the Baptist's suffering and death, and concludes that the Son of Man would have to suffer in the same way. Rather than striding in with glowing clothing, followed by a shining cloud, the road to Jesus' lordship followed the pattern of faithful John: Jesus was beaten and led to his own death, alone, on a different hillside—an event Peter could not comprehend even as it occurred.

When our expectations are for power on glowing mountaintops, we may well miss the kingdom of God in its moment of humble triumph.

Mariam Kamell
Postdoctoral Fellow, New Testament Studies
Regent College

Wearing Christ

Romans 13:11–14

How should Christians live? Paul answers, by approaching the advent in a deep way. The details of the advent on which we usually focus—the narrative of the birth, Mary, the shepherds, the wise men—what are they? Not symbols of abstract values, such as cheerfulness or hope, good will or peace. Christmas does not recur to remind us of these. In fact Christmas cannot recur, because it cannot return. It was a unique event in real time. As we live on, the advent recedes further into the past. But (Paul implies) Christ's coming is part of a process, part of a unique purpose. We ought not to try to recapture it. For Paul notes that the salvation of Christians, their final deliverance from the darkness of sin, is nearer now than when they first believed. And, by implication, nearer now than when the one in whom they trusted, the Word, was made flesh.

What then? Christ is not only to be admired, or celebrated, or worshipped. We must not stop at these. He is to be "put on." His is the character to "wear" as the darkness of a world into which Christ has come becomes light, and as "the day" draws near.

Paul Helm
Fifield, United Kingdom
Teaching Fellow, Theology and Philosophy
Regent College

Contemplative Prayer
Luke 2:21–39

This narrative of the recognition of the Christ by two senior citizens inspires us to finish well by persevering in the life of contemplative prayer. Anna and Simeon appear in the pages of revelation out of the obscurity that often characterizes true contemplatives. An encouragement for seniors in the community of God who often feel insignificant in their less active years, these two also inspire younger people to consult practised, contemplative seniors who are able to see things that others miss in the rush of life. People of every age who wish to "see Jesus" should note the features of contemplative prayer that Anna and Simeon model.

Contemplative prayer is *initiated and sustained by the Spirit* (vv. 25–27), and it is profoundly *informed by and responsive to Scripture.* Having encountered the living Word in the written Word, they were expecting him. Prayer is thus *responsive participation in the Triune God*, not a graceless discipline, issuing in rich worship (Simeon's canticle, vv. 29–32, and Anna's epitaph, vv. 37–38). *It incorporates all of life*—the revelations of listening prayer prompted their timely action (vv. 27, 28, and 38). Simeon's perception that the messianic mission includes suffering for both Jesus and his people (vv. 34–35) indicates that contemplative prayer *serves to normalize suffering in the kingdom of God.* Finally, *it* transforms us, evoking a thankful disposition toward God (v. 38) and a missional concern for neighbour (v. 32)—Simeon shows a rare awareness of the intended international horizon of Yahweh's purpose and the missional nature of his covenant people (v. 32).

Ross Hastings
Associate Professor, Mission Studies
Regent College

Silent Reflection

Luke 2:41–52

In spite of the various religious debates about her centrality in the Christmas story, Mary the mother of Jesus is a poignant figure.

An angel comes to meet her, gives her news that must have been overwhelming, and then provides reassurance that this is not an experience to be feared but one that indicates she is highly favoured. She goes through the experience of pregnancy, shares the joy with her cousin, Elizabeth, experiences the awkward chronology of how all this fits with virginity, has the child in a non-descript location, and watches shepherds worship her newborn.

In the early adolescent years of Jesus, she and her husband go through normal parental angst as he disappears for three days. Ironically, when they do find him and express their anxiety around the search, he wonders why they were looking for him and he gives them an answer they do not understand.

It makes perfect sense that in the midst of all this busyness, disruption, and confusion, "his mother treasured all these things in her heart" (v. 51). Silent reflection is a good posture when in the presence of God incarnate.

Rod J. K. Wilson
President; Professor, Counselling and Psychology
Regent College

The Adventure of Waiting Well

Matthew 25:14–30

The long-awaited infant became the rabbi Jesus, who taught of the second advent and the kingdom of heaven. His disciples were full of questions, and in Matthew 24 and 25 he tells them several different stories as answers. Now these same stories guide us, for even as we celebrate the birth that was, we too await the event that shall be. And as shown by the tale of the talents, we may have to reassess what we think waiting faithfully means.

In this tale, the servant who dares not to take risks is punished; the other two servants are lauded and called faithful because they use well what is given to them. Jesus then immediately clarifies with the next passage what it means to use well what the Master has placed in one's trust. His potent proclamation, that loving and serving God means actively loving and serving others, makes it plain that we must not mistake the parable as an encouragement to be "the best" at something, jeopardizing relational and community time: faithfulness clearly requires sacrificing being the best for these things. A daunting investment. This parable calls us to take risks in multiplying what God has entrusted—yet we are shown clearly in what follows that doing so cannot be at the cost of loving, and thus living, well. For what is, after all, the greatest gift we've been given to tend?

And, for the faithful, to bury that gift is simply not an option.

> "O Come all ye Faithful…. O come, let us adore him,
> Christ the Lord."

Kirstin Jeffrey Johnson
Tullins, France
PhD Candidate, University of St Andrews, Scotland
Regent Alum (MCS, 1998)

49

And Just Who Is This Family?

Matthew 25:31–46

Matthew chapter 24 records Jesus' teaching about his second advent; Matthew 25 tells us three stories of how to behave while we're waiting. Our text for this evening, the final part of the chapter, is retold beautifully by Leo Tolstoy in his story, "Where Love Is, There Is God Also" (retold again in *Shoemaker Martin*, a wonderful picture book for children by Bernadette Watts). As Tolstoy's title reminds us, when we show love to those around us, Jesus' family, we are not only bringing God's love into the life of the world, but we are also bringing in God himself who is love—and we are loving God.

And who is this family? It is the hungry, the sick, the homeless. An African minister asks us to read Matthew 25 over and over and then go the extra mile to discover just who some of Jesus' brothers and sisters are ("Experiencing Life at the Margins," *Christianity Today*, July 2006). He urges us: "Experience the situation of those on the margins. 'God so loved the world'—how dare we identify with him in that love if we don't go there, if we don't choose the margins?"

May our eyes be opened this Advent to the members of Jesus' family on the "margins." And may we learn how to love them. For each act of love becomes at once a re-enactment of God's "having come," a celebration of God-with-us, and an anticipation of the final coming—"His kingdom spread from shore to shore."

"Love that gives, gives evermore, gives with zeal, with eager hands, spares not, keeps not, all outpours, ventures all, it all expends."
(W. H. Vanstone)

Mary-Ruth K. Wilkinson
Sessional Lecturer
Regent College

Clarity of Sight

1 John 3:5–9; 4:9–10

Often the season of Advent can emerge as a blender-full of shopping lists, office parties, and parking stress—punctuated by a few religious moments. And against this backdrop of neon swirl, John's writing can seem starkly black and white. His talk of being born of God, doing what is right, foregoing sin's continued practice (or thereby leaguing with the devil) could shout "caricature" to our contemporary ears: our busy world replete with random "happy holidays" is too complex to profit from such affrontive clarity. Or is it?

When I risk sitting still with them, John's words blow through my mind, a crisp autumnal breeze. The foggy neon swirl recedes, and for a moment I can see: a sinner by default, I need this God whose black and white passion for his purpose—to move toward sinners and free us from sin's chronic pull toward death—embodies his great love for us. Perhaps then, this Advent season, we should seek to see with focused and unflinching eyes what's real about our lives, our sin, our hearts, our God. For if we can, we will then see—amid one thousand other lesser sights—the clear and joyous splendour of our Father's love, embodied in the Son he has sent.

Connally Gilliam
Arlington, Virginia
Writer, Author, and Life Coach
Regent Alum (DipCS, 1988)

Redemption Through Suffering

Isaiah 52:13–53:12

Sin is not redeemed by scrubbing it out of existence, but by taking it in as a sacrifice that justifies many (Isa. 53:11). This is obviously what Jesus did. We cannot do this in and of ourselves. But we can participate in what Jesus does with the sins of the world. He takes them. Suffers them.

We can enter the way of Jesus' cross and participate in Jesus' reconciliation of the world. This is a radical shift from condemning sin and sinners—an ugly business at best. We no longer stand around as disapproving spectators of the sins of others, but become participants in the sacrificial life of Jesus as he takes the sins of our children, the sins of our pastors, the sins of our friends, *our* sins.

Isaiah 53 requires a radical revision of our imaginations to take this in: to see sacrifice, offering, and suffering as essential, not an option, to salvation. This is most difficult to grasp—difficult for the Hebrews in Babylon, difficult for Christians anywhere. There is a fathomless mystery at the heart of this: making right by means of another, Another.

Eugene H. Peterson
Professor Emeritus, Spiritual Theology
Regent College

Praying with Honesty
Luke 1:5–17

Zechariah and his wife, Elizabeth, had been faithfully living, serving the Lord. But they had no children, and they were old. When Zechariah entered the temple, he encountered the angel saying, "Do not be afraid, Zechariah; your prayer has been heard" (v. 13).

God knew Zechariah and remembered all the prayers that he poured out before God. He had been with him in every moment of his journey. God did not ignore him. He had heard Zechariah's very personal prayer. At the same time, at a deeper level, Zechariah's prayer and anguish were connecting and representing all of humanity, who had been waiting and longing for the child who brings salvation to the world. God's answer for Zechariah's prayer was manifested in the birth of John the Baptist, who prepared the hearts of people for the coming of Christ. This answer to Zechariah's personal prayer wonderfully became the answer for the deep longing of the entire creation.

God knows each of us by name. He notices the depths of our desire, and he invites us to pray a very personal prayer. He is attentive to us. In his grace, and in his time, our prayer will be answered in a surprising way.

Lord, give me courage to be honest with you
and to be open to you.
Help me to trust in you, so that by your grace, I may wait for you.

Fumiko Hiraga
Iruma City, Japan
Lecturer, Obirin University and Musashino University
Regent Alum (MCS, 2002)

An Eager "Yes" to the Grace of God

Luke 1:26–38

"Greetings, you who are highly favoured! The Lord is with you" (v. 28). What can this incredible announcement mean? The reply of the angel is that Mary has been favoured and will be with child. And here, in the presence of this angel, Mary must make a choice. As a virgin she will conceive a child, and this child will be the ruler of the kingdom of God. How will she respond? The church has always loved these words: "I am the Lord's servant. May your word to me be fulfilled" (v. 38).

"Then the angel left her," we read. What the angel recognized is that there was no more to be said. She had responded fully and completely to the call of God. In so doing, she was a vehicle of God's saving work and a perfect model or image of what it means to respond to that call. With her "yes," Mary embodies two realities: the grace of God, and the appropriate response to that grace. While we affirm the priority of God's grace, her consent is not incidental. Mary shows us that true discipleship requires a response.

Her road was different from ours. But as we celebrate the incarnation through Mary's womb, let us consider what God may be saying to us. May we have a renewed appreciation of God's grace to us. And may we also have the courage to act, to choose to respond with our own "yes" to the call of God.

Gordon T. Smith
Mayne Island, BC
President, reSource Leadership International
Sessional Lecturer, Regent College

Mary's Song, Our Song

Luke 1:39–56

Mary's song—the "Magnificat"—is our song. It is the definitive Advent carol we should sing as we anticipate the advent of the one who comes to deliver us from tyranny, oppression, and sin. But Mary's song is more than just a song of deliverance. It is also a prediction of the failure and downfall of the proud, powerful, and rich. This is what makes singing this definitive Advent carol so difficult. For Mary's advent song seems to grate against the wealth and power of Western society, particularly during the Christmas "shopping season."

But as Christians we are called to identify with Mary who bears witness to the coming of Jesus the Messiah, who overthrows the dominant values of our world and rescues the poor and the marginalized from their tyranny. Mary's song reminds us that the "good news" of Christ's advent is not just about our spiritual rebirth through his life, death, and resurrection, but also the real and material liberation of those on the margins—the poor, the hungry, and the outcasts. And as such, Mary's song needs to become our song throughout the entire year, not just during Advent.

Mary's song is a hard song to sing with honesty and sincerity. But God's Holy Spirit came upon Mary and inspired her to sing. May that same Spirit continually "come upon" us and inspire us to renounce what keeps us so far from the kingdom of God—those utterly human values of power, vanity, and materialism.

Bob Derrenbacker
Sudbury, ON
President; Provost, Thorneloe University
Former Assistant Professor, New Testament
Regent College

A Slow Faithfulness

Luke 1:57–80

Mary is one of our paradigmatic examples of faith—faced with what was likely to be a shameful and humiliating act of obedience, we see her immediately and wholeheartedly embrace the call of God. Zechariah's response to his own angelic visitation is, I think, more typical, more human—more like me. Where Mary's response is swift and unqualified, Zechariah struggles to believe, struggles to accept the promises of God, even coming from an angel—after all, they're both so old! Zechariah's faithful response does come, but it is drawn out and painful, slowly growing through those pregnant months of silence, waiting for the arrival of the promised one. Zechariah is where most of us live most of our lives: slow to believe; struggling with our muted, stunted responses to the grace of God. But the hope here is that Zechariah does get there in the end—when he is finally unsilenced, he, like Mary, finds praise pouring out of his mouth. Mary and Zechariah take different paths to faithfulness—one immediate, one slow and hard—but they end up in a similar place: both filled with the Spirit, caught up in praise of God, and surrendered to what God is doing. Zechariah finishes his song glorying in One who leads us, "showing us the way, one foot at a time, down the path of peace" (v. 79, *The Message*).

Robyn L. Wrigley-Carr
Sydney, Australia
Lecturer in Spirituality, Australian College of Ministries
Regent Alum (MCS, 1998)

On Bended Knee

Matthew 2:1–12

I once stood in Durham cathedral and felt drawn to bow down upon my knees. The only problem was that I worried what other people might think of me. Walking around admiring the building, I blended in like all the other tourists. Bowing would make me stick out like a pious fool. In truth, I was already bowing—to expectations, real and imagined, of people who were oblivious to my well-being. I was performing before an invisible audience, unable to worship the God who longed to set me free.

How striking is the freedom the wise men possessed in the face of intimidating circumstances. Upon entering Jerusalem, no mention is made of how mighty the city looks, how great are her buildings, or how holy is the temple. Instead the Magi ask: "Where is the one who has been born king of the Jews? We saw *his* star when it rose and have come to worship *him*" (Matt. 2:2, italics mine). Before Herod, no mention is made of any ambassadorial gifts. There is no respectful bowing down. All of that is saved for a child.

Matt Canlis
Pitlochry, Scotland
Pastor, Church of Scotland
Regent Alum (MDiv, 2000)

An Advent Prayer

1 John 1:1–2:2

Lord Jesus Christ,
Your first disciples heard, saw, and touched you. They concluded that you are the very life—the essence—of God. You are eternal life. Yet they never forgot this crucial fact: you are also flesh and blood.

In this passage you call us to be gripped by the knowledge that the fullness of God lives in your human body. And you live in us!

Too easily we lose touch with this reality. Too easily you become a pious name, an abstract idea, a theological term. Too often we talk about you as if you are not present with us. (But though we cannot see you with our eyes, you are near.) Lord, have mercy on us, sinners.

Grant us, Lord Jesus, during this Advent season, the grace to contemplate you as the Incarnate One. In you, there is no darkness, no sin, no loneliness. You are light.

So we desire this same integrity that you embody in flesh and spirit. As we contemplate you, O God-made-flesh, may you dry up the roots of our sin and transform our inner lives into the likeness of you.

Amen.

Alvin S. B. Ung
Kuala Lumpur, Malaysia
Writer and Teacher
Regent Alum (MCS, 2006)

Living Toward a Vision

Revelation 22:1–5

We all live toward some vision of the future. It is part of what makes us human; we are creatures that *long*. Here, at the far end of the biblical story, John gives us such a vision.

It is not only a river that flows through these verses, but a tapestry—a weaving together of the holy longings of God's people through history. We have not always known its name, but ever since we were exiled from the garden we have desired this coming city: its healing, its peace, and its justice. We have longed for the presence of God, to see him face to face and not die.

As Christ-followers, we live toward this vision.

Sometimes.

There is another city shaped by desire. John calls it Babylon. Its desire is for itself and its own glory. It is every city, society, moment, or thought opposed to the will of God and his kingdom.

Babylon is demanding and immediate. But Babylon is a lesser thing: it has rivers, but they are places of weeping (Ps. 137); it is a home to nations, but not the place of their healing (Rev. 14:8).

For which city does your heart long?

At Advent we remind ourselves that we are a people waiting. We remember the king, who became an infant, who was a lamb. And this lamb sits on the throne at the centre of the city of God. We will see him one day, face to face. And we will not die.

Amen. Come, Lord Jesus.

Andrew Shamy
Auckland, New Zealand
Director, Compass Foundation NZ
Regent Alum (MCS, 2008)

Meaning and Destiny
Daniel 2

Nebuchadnezzar was troubled by a dream. It was a grand, dazzling dream: a dream about the future, about destiny, and about the end of the world. But he didn't know what it meant. No facile psycho-babble would suffice as explanation and, just to be sure, Nebuchadnezzar required that the interpreter also know the dream without being told it. It was revealed to Daniel's prayer meeting: Christ is the ruler and end of human history. It is God who validates and gives meaning to Nebuchadnezzar's kingship, who is directing it and all human history toward its end, Jesus Christ.

As Chesterton has written, the Christ who came on that first Christmas is the "Everlasting Man" who fulfils all the longings of human culture and history. In him alone is found meaning and destiny for our lives. But this wonderful message needs a messenger. We, like Daniel, find ourselves living in exile, serving a culture that worships foreign gods. Like Daniel, our call is to be in our culture, not removed from it, to learn the language and literature of the "Babylonians," and to become interpreters of our society's dreams. All around us are dreamers searching for meaning. The Christ we proclaim is the one of whom we sing, "The hopes and fears of all the years are met in thee tonight."

Paul S. Williams
David J. Brown Family Associate Professor of Marketplace Theology
Regent College

Merry Christmas!

John 1:1–18

What a text for Christmas Day! The Word whom John says "was God," through whom the whole universe was made, has become what he was not—has become one of us. Have you ever heard anything so utterly fantastic?

Why does John declare this wonderful Christmas gospel using the term Word, or, as it is in Greek, *Logos*? Why not begin the story, "In the beginning was the Son, and the Son was with God, and the Son was God"? Or why not begin the story, "In the beginning was King?" Why, "In the beginning was the Word?"

Because John is first and foremost an evangelist. By using the term "Word" he is able to connect with the widest scope of his contemporaries. For his Greek friends, Word, or Logos, referred variously to "that-which-gives-order-and-coherence-to-life," and "that-which-makes-life-go-round." For his Jewish friends, Word, or Logos, referred variously to "the-speech-by-which-we-know-the-invisible-God," and "the-performative-word-which-brought-the-universe-into-being." Can you imagine how both of John's sets of friends were set back on their heels by the startling thing he claims? Whatever it was they thought the Word was has now become one of us!

And why does John bring us to this incredible affirmation and then say, "We have seen his glory?" (v. 14). Why does he not say, "And the Word became flesh and God and humans were reconciled?" Or, why not say, "And the Word became flesh, and the powers of sin, evil, and death were defeated?" Why, "We have seen his glory?"

Because for John that is the wonder of the story. Glory simply means "that-which-makes-God-be-God." It is what Moses wanted to see on the mountain top—"show me your glory" (Exod. 33:18). He wants to know the very essence of who God is and what God is

61

like. He wants to know what makes God tick, and therefore, what makes what God makes tick. So do I. So do you. Oh, the wonder! In the flesh of Jesus of Nazareth, God answers this deepest longing of the human heart. In Jesus, God, now in our flesh, shows us what makes God be God.

So, read on. In one of the four gospels. Read on into the life and ministry of this one who has come and is to come and comes even today. Choose to spend the beginning months of the new year reading through Matthew, Mark, Luke, or John, and you will find yourself not only startled, but back on your heels. You will find yourself drawn to your knees. Who would have ever dreamed up such a God?

Merry Christmas!

> "Let all mortal flesh keep silence,
> and with fear and trembling stand;
> ponder nothing earthly minded,
> for with blessing in his hand,
> Christ our God to earth descendeth,
> our full homage to demand."

Darrell W. Johnson
Vancouver, British Columbia
Pastor, First Baptist Church
Former Associate Professor, Pastoral Theology
Regent College

CPSIA information can be obtained at www.ICGtesting.com
Printed in the USA
LVOW080548291011

252570LV00002B/1/P

9 781573 834544